New York

Adventures

New York City
Adventures

Donna Vann

CF4·K

Dedicated to God's "secret agents,"
who work tirelessly to bring his love
to the people of
New York City.

10 9 8 7 6 5 4 3 2 1

© Copyright 2010 Donna Vann
ISBN: 978-1-84550-546-2

Published in 2010
by
Christian Focus Publications,
Geanies House, Fearn, Tain,
Ross-shire, IV20 1TW,
Great Britain

Cover design by Daniel van Straaten
Cover illustration by Graham Kennedy
Other illustrations by Fred Apps
Printed by MPG Books Ltd, Bodmin, Cornwall

Scripture quotations are taken from the Holy Bible,
New Living Translation, copyright ©1996.
Used by permission of Tyndale House Publishers, Inc.,
Wheaton, Illinois 60189. All rights reserved.

Contents

In the Big Apple

Honk-honk-honk! Beep!

You feel like an insect crawling down the center of an enormous canyon. You're too busy gazing up at the soaring skyscrapers to watch where you're going. Look out! Better wait for the green light before you cross the street.

"Hey there! What's going on?"

Is that man yelling at you? No, he's calling a greeting to a lady who sells jewelry at a sidewalk stand. She shouts back, and the two carry on a friendly conversation. Everyone talks so loudly here, it seems!

There are loud smells, too, from sidewalk stands selling hot dogs, pretzels, roasted nuts, ice cream and more. Mix that all together with exhaust from buses and yellow taxis, plus the occasional stinky whiff rising up from the drains. Your ears and nose hardly know how to take it all in.

You've arrived in The Big Apple – New York City. It's like nowhere else on earth.

You cross the street and continue down the sidewalk. Sirens echo off buildings and people rush past, speaking in a jumble of foreign languages. Are they tourists, like yourself? Some are, but many are residents. Over 170 languages are spoken here. Two out of every three New Yorkers either came here from another country, or their parents did.

Everyone seems to know where they're going and wants to get there in a hurry. You pick up the pace. There's a rhythm to this city that gets inside you, makes you want to speed up too.

Then you turn a corner and find yourself beside a leafy park, where dog owners chat quietly while their dogs play together. In this bold, brash city you don't expect to see peaceful parks or neighborhoods which feel like small towns. Yet they exist all over the five boroughs of New York.

You may be surprised to find people who are quietly trusting God with their lives and trying to make a difference in the lives of others. You will meet some of them in this book.

So why not take a few bites out of The Big Apple, and taste the real New York City!

Secrets of the City

New York is rightly called "the city that never sleeps." There are exciting and surprising things to do here at any hour of the day or night.

You can tour the city by helicopter or hire a classic car with a driver to escort you around. Or you might take a fast speedboat ride out to the Statue of Liberty. Did you forget to bring a camera? No problem, just hire your own personal photographer to follow you around for the day and record your visit.

Do you like sports? Well, why not take a kayak out on the Hudson River, or learn to fly on a trapeze overlooking Manhattan harbor. Maybe you'd rather go scuba diving in the East River, or rent some fishing tackle and fish in Central Park lake.

You might hold a sleepover at the Museum of Natural History, where you and your friends can roam through the darkened halls with flashlights. (Don't worry, the exhibits don't really come alive as they do in the movie *Night at the Museum!*) After sundown in the summer, you can watch movies outdoors in parks, on rooftops or under the Brooklyn Bridge.

Speaking of the Brooklyn Bridge, one of the most unique things to do in New York is to walk across it. You climb a ramp to reach a broad walkway above the traffic – but watch out for speeding cyclists. It's a great way to get some exercise and amazing views of Manhattan.

Are you fond of dogs? New Yorkers love theirs. As you ride the subway you may spot an elegantly dressed woman carrying a small dog in her designer handbag. If you happen to be in the city on Halloween, visit Tompkins Square Park in the East Village for a bizarre sight. It's the Halloween Dog Parade! Owners bring their dogs dressed up as pirates, firemen, Indians, playing cards or just about anything else you can imagine. The dogs probably don't enjoy this as much as their owners do.

If there's anything fascinating or fun that you can't do here, it's just because no one has thought of it yet. And then there's the famous New York food…

Wake up in the middle of the night desperate for a little snack? If you live downtown, you can order a freshly baked warm chocolate chip cookie delivered to your door. Or you can head out onto the streets and find any kind of restaurant you're in the mood for. Feel like Thai food at two in the morning? You'll find something open, whether it's ethnic food from the various cultures of the city, or maybe just a frozen yogurt to cool you down on warm summer nights. It's all available twenty-four hours a day.

On the other hand if you decide to sleep in late, why not go for that classic New York tradition, brunch. Brunch is served around 11 a.m. and is a hearty combination of breakfast and lunch. You can order an omelet with wild ingredients like avocado or lobster, or a toasted bagel with cream cheese. Oh, and maybe a nice fruit smoothie to drink. Yummy!

One important secret to learn in any new city is how to get around. It's easy to find your way here, as the streets of Manhattan run parallel. The main exception is Broadway, which cuts across at an angle. This angle created a triangular patch of land on which the tallest building in the world was built. At least, the tallest for 1902. With twenty-three stories it looks low today, but it is still impressive.

The so-called "Flatiron Building" was constructed around a steel frame, the kind used today in all skyscrapers. Its sharp point at the front looked like an iron used to press clothes. It was a wonder in its time – passersby made bets on how far it would fall once the wind blew it over! Some didn't want to walk too close, just in case.

As you're walking around the city, if you pause on the sidewalk looking lost, a New Yorker will probably stop and politely offer help. However, if you look confident of where you are going, be prepared for other tourists to stop you and ask for directions! And there's more than a chance you will bump into one of your favorite actors while waiting to cross a street, or that you'll get to watch a movie or TV series being filmed.

Another surprise awaits underground. When you head below to ride the subway, you might not expect to find anything other than dust and dirt and noise. The first subway was built in 1904.

Now it has over 600 miles of tracks that will take you anywhere you want to go.

But while you are down there, look around. At dozens of stations, you'll find paintings or sculptures or mosaics. You could spend all day visiting the subway art "gallery". There is even a subway art guide on the web, so you know what to look for. You'll also see bands playing and magicians performing. As you ride the subway you will be crushed up next to people from all cultures and walks of life. It feels pretty wild down there but it's all part of the New York scene.

The city is full of secret surprises. Inside busy Grand Central Station on 42nd Street you might think a whisper could never be heard above the noise. Yet in this vast arched building, there is a place below the main hall where you can talk in whispers. You stand in one corner facing the wall, and have a friend stand in the opposite corner facing the wall. Your whispers are transmitted back and forth across the arched ceiling, as if you were using walkie-talkies.

THINGS TO SEE AND DO

- Grand Central Station – East 42nd Street at Park Avenue.
- Subway art.
- Flatiron Building – West 23rd at Fifth Avenue.

One secret of the city which you may not have thought of – what happens to all the garbage? When author Charles Dickens visited New York in 1842, he saw pigs gobbling up garbage in the streets. Today, garbage collectors known as "New York's Strongest" haul away 50,000 tons of trash every day, put out by the eight million residents. That's the number of people living in the five boroughs of the city: Manhattan, Brooklyn, Queens, the Bronx and Staten Island. Once the trash is collected, it's crushed and compacted, then sent miles away to be buried in a landfill.

I wonder what happens with your garbage? I don't mean the kind that's put out on the street for the trash man. We all have a lot of "junk" in our lives – things we've done or said that hurt others, for example. How do we get rid of the bad stuff inside us? Do we just ignore it, let it pile up and hope nobody notices?

We don't have to do that, because God has a better idea. First, let's think about who God is. Maybe you have heard his name used as a swear word. That makes people forget there really is a God who made the world. He's everywhere all at the same time and sees everything we think and do. He rules over the whole universe.

Often people don't want God to rule over them. They think they can do a good job running their own lives without him. In spite of that, God wants to be the leader of our lives, not because he's bossy, but because he made us and loves us very much. He knows exactly what's best for us. We'll learn more about this in the next chapter.

Along with being "the city that never sleeps," you may have heard New York City called "The Big Apple". You might wonder if they grow apples here, or if you will see folks walking down the street eating apples.

No, it was jazz musicians who made the phrase popular. In the 1920s and 30s when jazz was sweeping America, they wanted to play where the best musicians were. New York was the place to be, and they called it The Big Apple. The phrase was used again by the tourist office in the 1970s, when there was a lot of crime in the city. The idea was to make tourists think of a healthy apple when they thought of New York. Today the city is one of the safest anywhere, but the name stuck. All over the world New York is known as The Big Apple.

In the next chapter, we will take a trip back in time and meet some New Yorkers who lived here even before there were streets.

Only One Life

Your father and other men of your tribe have felled one of the canoe-making trees. You and your friends follow along as they carry the tree down to the riverbank. They will let it rest for three moons until it is dry. Then they will burn the center with fire and hollow it out to make a canoe. The tribe needs many canoes to get back and forth from the mainland to this hilly island where they spend the summers. Fish and oysters are plentiful here, and there are bear and many other game to hunt.

Suddenly the men stop. They set the tree down and begin talking in whispers. Your father motions for you to stay back. What is going on? You and your best friend creep around the tree and hide behind some bushes.

There on the shore stands the chief of your tribe and his top warriors. Other men are there too, strange men with pale skins and hair on their faces. They are wearing what look like buckets on their heads, and many dark clothes which cover their bodies completely. They must be very hot.

The chief of the white men hands your chief some bright beads. Laid out on the ground on a piece of cloth are some tools. You have never seen such tools and don't know what they are for. Your chief takes the beads and the white men nod their heads, looking pleased.

That was the scene four centuries ago, when the Dutchman Peter Minuit bought the island of Manhattan from the local tribes, for a few tools and trinkets. At least, he thought he was buying it. These native Americans probably thought he was buying hunting rights. They may not have understood they were giving him the right to own the island.

Today, if you travel to the northern tip of Manhattan, where the Hudson River and Harlem River meet, you arrive at a beautiful wilderness area called Inwood Hill Park. When you step into the forest, you are in a different world. Instead of noisy city streets, you walk on a path surrounded by green and the song of birds. The trees rise like leafy skyscrapers around you. You are in the world of the original native Americans, the first New Yorkers.

Rangers are on hand to guide you along the paths through the thick forest, past rocky caves where these early dwellers took shelter. The Indians liked to build their canoes from the tulip-poplar trees found here. These tall trees with their straight trunks were ideal for the purpose. A boulder with a bronze plaque on the shore of the Harlem River marks the spot where Minuit supposedly met the Indians.

From this northern edge of Manhattan, an Indian trail ran all the way down the island to the southern tip. Today we know it as Broadway. The Dutch decided to build their settlement called New Amsterdam at the south end of the trail, overlooking the water.

To keep out possible attacks from the British or Indians in the rest of the island, the Dutch put up a protecting wall on the north side of their town. It was made of wooden logs twelve feet long and sharpened at the upper end. The street alongside it became a main road with shops, the city hall and a church. Now it seems tiny and cramped, yet it is the most famous street in the world. Can you guess its name?

This is Wall Street, where men used to gather under a tree to make business deals. Now it's the home of the New York Stock Exchange. It seems funny that such an important place would be named for a wooden fence.

The Dutch colony struggled for several years with Indian wars and bungling governors. In 1664 the British invaded, and the Dutch didn't bother putting up a fight. New Amsterdam was renamed New York, in honor of the Duke of York. The city continued to grow and thrive.

During the colonies' war for independence from Britain, New York City played a key role. However, the city was not eager to enter the war. But suddenly the British navy appeared off the

---

THINGS TO SEE AND DO
- Inwood Hill Park – Metro A to 207th Street.
- New York Stock Exchange – corner of Wall Street and Broad Street.
- Statue of George Washington on the steps of the Federal Building where he was inaugurated president – across from the Stock Exchange.

coast of Staten Island. The British knew if they could capture New York, they'd have a good harbor and could drive a wedge between the colonies.

The colonial army under Commander George Washington was camped in the north of Manhattan, in what is now Harlem. Washington knew the British planned to attack and take over the whole of Manhattan, but he had no information on when and where the attack would take place.

Volunteers were needed. Who would go behind enemy lines as a spy, and get the information?

At first, no one spoke up. You might wonder why. Doesn't being a secret agent sound exciting and important? At that time however, spying was looked on as shameful. No one who was a gentleman would do such a dishonorable thing. Finally one man volunteered – a young captain from Connecticut. His name was Nathan Hale.

Nathan Hale had been working as a schoolteacher when the war broke out in 1775. He was a handsome man, good at sports. Those who knew him liked his honest character. He didn't want to be a spy, but he wanted to serve his country. That September, he reluctantly agreed to cross into Long Island and spy on the British.

Nathan disguised himself as a schoolmaster and went behind enemy lines. Probably an open and honest man like Nathan was not well suited to being a spy. Before he managed to get any information, the British invaded Manhattan and he was captured. He was sentenced to hang.

The next morning, this brave 21-year-old stood before a small group of British soldiers near the Dove Tavern (close to what is now the corner of Third Avenue and 66th Street). He'd had a good life, but it was about to be over.

Nathan gave a speech before he was hanged. According to witnesses he said, "I only regret that I have but one life to lose for my country." His courage impressed the British. Here was a man who thought his country was worth dying for. He was willing to face a disgraceful death, and he did it with dignity and courage.

Many centuries before Nathan Hale, another young teacher stood condemned to die. Like Nathan, he was admired by his comrades. His death was also disgraceful, yet he faced it with courage. His name was Jesus of Nazareth.

Several things marked Jesus out as being one-of-a-kind. He did miracles of healing and fed thousands of people from a few fish and loaves of bread. He also brought the dead back to life.

And then there was his teaching. "We've never heard anyone teach like this," his listeners said (Matthew 7:28-29). But he didn't just tell them about God. He told them that he was God. Some people got very angry about this, and decided to execute him. Jesus was killed by crucifixion, which was a long and painful death on a cross.

Jesus was God's only son, sent to earth to live among humans and show them what God was like. He was the only person who has ever lived the perfect life. It's hard to imagine, but he never did, said or thought anything wrong. Yet he was accused of stirring up trouble and crucified. If he really was God's son, why didn't God send down an angel army to save him?

God could have done that, but he didn't. It was all part of his plan. God knows we tend to go our own way and mess things up. Yet he loves every one of us – he's the one who made us. He wants to get to know us, but our wrongdoing stands in the way. Someone was needed, to take the punishment we deserved. That someone was Jesus.

Remember in the last chapter, we talked about garbage. Every one of us has garbage that we drag around with us – all our wrong thoughts and words and actions. It's like having a huge black trash bag filled with all the bad stuff in our lives. The Bible calls this bad stuff "sin". Imagine trying to drag this huge bag everywhere we go!

But God sent Jesus so we don't have to do that. He wants to forgive us completely. He will take that trash bag with all our garbage and vaporize it. Pow – it's gone! We don't have to carry it around any more.

Like Nathan Hale, Jesus had only one earthly life. He gave it up, not for his country, but for you and me, so that we could be freed from our guilt. He only asks that we turn away from our sin and follow him. That means believing in him with our whole hearts and being willing to obey him.

Maybe you have not yet told Jesus that you believe in him and want to be forgiven. If not, you can talk to him about it. You can use your own words, because he understands what you're trying to say. Just thank him that he died for all the wrong things you have thought and said and done. Ask him to help you be the kind of person he wants you to be. And don't forget to thank him that he has forgiven you and made you part of his family forever.

If you have prayed to put your faith in Jesus, it would be good to tell someone else about it. You might tell a parent or the person who gave you this book.

Becoming a follower of Jesus is the most exciting thing that can ever happen to anyone! As you read this book, you will encounter New Yorkers who have put their trust in Jesus and followed him in remarkable ways.

But let's move ahead another century, where we'll travel on a railroad without any rails.

What Can One Person Do?

It's the middle of the night. You're creeping along the edge of a ploughed field behind your mother and brother. Your brother whispers something but your mother shushes him quickly. Now all you can hear is the gentle strumming of crickets. Sweat is pouring down your face. What if someone wakes up and finds you gone? The three of you are slaves. You belong to the owner of the big house you left behind. He's a cruel master. You pray silently he will never find you.

Ten miles to go. Your mother knows of a "station" in the next town, a house where you will be hidden and given food. She said there are some white people who will take care of you. They will give you food, hide you during the day and then tell you the way to the next safe house after dark. But you know your master keeps bloodhounds. Won't they be able to pick up your trail?

You're near a bridge over a little creek when you have an idea. "Mama!" you whisper. "Let's wade across the creek! Then the hounds can't track us."

Your mother nods and leads your sister into the shallow water. You follow with a sigh of relief. For now, you are safe, but there are many days and many miles to go before you reach Canada.

For many years, Africans had been transported across the Atlantic to work on large cotton plantations in the South. They were brought in ships under horrible conditions, and then sold to landowners once they reached America. Families were often split up, with husbands, wives and children sold to different plantations, never to see each other again.

Throughout the 1800s, some slaves were able to escape from the plantations by fleeing on the Underground Railroad. This was not a railroad with rail tracks and train cars, but a network of secret paths and safe houses. Slaves could move across the U.S. to freedom in Canada, Mexico, or into northern states where they would try to blend in.

The way the railroad worked was this: "conductors" on the railroad were people who would help the fleeing slaves. They took them into their homes and taught them secret codes so they could find the next "stations". These were the safe houses along the route. The slaves would make their way at night from station to station, often hiding in barns or sheds, protected by whites who knew that slavery was wrong. If they were caught helping the slaves they were fined or put in prison.

New York City played a key role in the Underground Railroad. Henry Ward Beecher, pastor of Plymouth Church in Brooklyn, spoke out strongly against slavery. The church itself was nicknamed the "Grand Central Depot" of the Underground Railroad.

Slaves were probably hidden in the large basement of the church, which had no outside entrances. They would have slept on the floor and had chamber pots for toilets. Food and warm clothing would be given to them for their journey northward. But there was no running water or electricity, and candles were a fire hazard. It must have been very dark and spooky hiding there at night.

In spite of that, it was an excellent location. The church was only a few short blocks from the East River harbor. Slaves could easily walk that distance under cover of darkness to ships which would take them to freedom in Canada.

Pastor Beecher did outlandish things to attract attention to the slavery problem. He even held mock auctions of slaves from the pulpit! He did this to make people aware of what was happening. When the congregation donated the purchase price for a slave, he or she would be set free.

Over the years, many famous anti-slavery heroes including Abraham Lincoln attended Plymouth Church. In more recent history, Rev. Dr. Martin Luther King, Jr. preached an early version of his "I have a Dream" speech there.

THINGS TO SEE AND DO
- Plymouth Church of the Pilgrims – 75 Hicks Street, Brooklyn - phone the church to arrange a tour.
- In Pursuit of Freedom – proposed historical walking tour of Brooklyn.

One of the most unusual speakers at the church was a tall black woman who had been a slave for 40 years, but was now free. In 1843 she felt God wanted her to travel around America and preach against slavery. Her original name was Isabella but she changed it to Sojourner Truth. A "sojourner" is someone who travels from place to place. Her second name "Truth" showed she always wanted to speak what was true.

Sojourner never learned to read and write, yet she was an entertaining and powerful speaker. She obeyed God and went out, even though at that time women were not accepted as public speakers. In addition to that, she was black. That meant she would automatically be looked down on by some in her audience. She could bring her listeners to tears as she preached for the rights of women and slaves and prisoners.

This courageous woman could have told God "no". She might have said, "Who am I, Lord, just one black woman. There is no way I can leave my home and travel all around the country preaching to white folks!" But she didn't argue with God. It took a lot of nerve, but she obeyed him and set out. As a result, many people changed their thinking about slavery.

A few years before, another New Yorker said "yes" to God. His action set something in motion that changed the lives of people around the world.

The scene was a lecture room at the Dutch Reformed Church on Fulton Street. Jeremiah Lanphier took out his pocket watch. Already thirty minutes past the hour of 12 noon, and no one had come! He sat alone, surrounded by a dozen empty wooden chairs.

He wanted to make a space and time for businessmen to stop and pray during the lunch hour. New York City in 1857 was a bustling place, filled with busy people trying their best to get ahead in life. Jeremiah had seen from the empty faces he passed in the street, that they needed God. He had prayed, "Lord, what would you have me do?" The answer, he felt, was to advertise a place and time for prayer.

But now it seemed he had misunderstood the answer. Not one person showed up. He was disappointed. Did God want him to pray all by himself? Just then he heard steps on the stairs. A man came through the door, asking if this was the prayer meeting. A few minutes later another arrived, until there were six men altogether. Led by Jeremiah, they began to pray.

A handful of men sitting in a room for a few minutes, praying – that doesn't sound very exciting. The next Wednesday, the number doubled. And the week after it doubled again. The idea of a weekly prayer meeting turned into a daily one. Every day from noon to one o'clock, people gathered in the Fulton Street room for prayer. At first only men attended, but soon women came too.

Before long, rich and poor, old and young, New Yorkers from every level of society began meeting for lunchtime prayer. Other churches took up the idea, but they were too small for the crowds.

Thousands began to gather in public halls and theaters. All over the city, New Yorkers were standing up to say how God had touched their lives and changed them. Many of these busy city-dwellers had had no room for God in their lives. They had never known or else forgotten that God sent Jesus to forgive them and give them new life. Every day more and more told how God had cleansed them of their sin and given them a relationship with himself.

Everyone in the city heard about it, as newspapers began to print daily reports on this surprising interest in prayer. This incredible movement became known as the "Fulton Street Revival". It spread from New York to many places around America, then to Ireland, Wales, Scotland and England. At the peak of the revival, around 10,000 New Yorkers every week were standing up to ask God's forgiveness for their wrong thoughts and actions.

Like Sojourner Truth, Henry Ward Beecher and the conductors on the Underground Railroad, Jeremiah Lanphier was an individual who followed God and made a difference. He could have told God "no". He might have said, "What if no one comes? That would be too embarrassing." But he simply obeyed God, and God did the rest.

What about today? Coney Island along Brooklyn's south shore is famous for its amusement parks and roller coasters. It even claims to be where the American hot dog was born! But the area has an unpleasant side. For years, hundreds of homeless people lived underneath the tall wooden beach boardwalk. They used wires to steal electricity from the lampposts, and fires were common. The wooden slats above their heads had spaces between them, so they were only small protection from the rain.

One of the homeless under the Coney Island boardwalk was a young woman named Debbe Santiago. She lived there in the sand and rubble, putting up with the rats that scurried around her in the night.

When Debbe came to understand how completely Jesus had forgiven her, she knew she wanted to tell everyone around her about him. But she also knew what the homeless were like – they

didn't trust anyone. They had no self-respect and no hope in their lives. They needed to see that God loved them before they'd be ready to hear about him.

So Debbe began to give food and clothing to the homeless, even before she had a home of her own. When she did find a place to live, she immediately used her home as a place where the homeless could take showers, eat and learn from the Bible. From that small start, a whole outreach to the homeless grew up.

Now Salt and Sea Mission feeds thousands of homeless at Coney Island each month. They provide all sorts of services, from handing out mail to helping people train for jobs. Bible classes and prayer meetings are held nearly every day. All this started because one young woman said "yes" when God challenged her to follow him.

While we are here on earth, God has something special in mind for each of us. Even though you are only one person, God hand-picked you to belong to him. He does not think you are too young or too anything to do what he has in mind for you! And he doesn't expect you to do it without his help. You may not know right away what God's design for your life is, but you can count on him to show you at the proper time.

In the next chapter, we'll meet a very large lady who has welcomed visitors to New York City for over 120 years.

Coming to America

Imagine your family are immigrants, coming to America from your home country of Ireland. The small steamship chugs into New York harbor. Everyone leans over the side, trying to peer through the fog. The ship's horn booms above your heads.

"There she is!" your sister shouts.

"Where?"

"I can't see anything!" But then you do. Looming out of the haze is a gigantic statue. The figure with her pale green robes is so tall, your ship feels like a toy bobbing below her. High above her head she holds a torch.

"She's got spikes sticking out of her head," says your sister.

"They look like rays of light to me."

"That's Lady Liberty," says your dad.

You're finally here!

It's been a long and grueling journey. Twelve days ago you and your family left the shores of Ireland, where you had always lived. But there was nothing to eat there, no work for your dad.

And now, after days of tossing and pitching on the rough seas, with everyone being sick, you are about to land in America! Your aunt and uncle will be waiting to welcome you.

But there are more adventures before you get to see them. Your steamship docks in New York Harbor and the passengers are told they must board another ship.

"Are they sending us back to Ireland?" you ask your dad.

"No, of course not," he replies, giving your shoulder a squeeze. "They're taking us to the immigration station to register us. It's only because we're poor – they want to check us out. Then we'll be able to enter New York City."

You clutch your suitcase and crowd into the transfer barge for Ellis Island, where immigrants go to register. Everyone is carrying something – bundles, bags, babies. It's bitterly cold, but you don't feel a thing. You're wearing three layers of clothes to save room in your suitcase. No one has had a bath in days and you are crammed in with other smelly unwashed bodies. But you don't care. A few moments ago you felt worn out but now the excitement is building. What will New York be like? Will it be a good place to live?

Your sister is sagging with exhaustion. She leans on your dad and almost drops her suitcase. He quickly tucks it under his arm and nudges her forward across the wooden gangplank to the shore of Ellis Island. Your mother is carrying the baby and trying to keep your little brother from running off. Along with everyone else from your ship, you enter the impressive building. You all drop your luggage in a huge pile inside and begin climbing the long staircase to the next floor of the immigration station.

By now your sister's eyelids are drooping and she can barely put one foot in front of another. You notice several men at the top of the stairs, staring down at the arriving passengers. Sometimes as a person walks past, one of the men makes a mark on the immigrant's coat with chalk. What's that for, you wonder?

Finally your family reaches the head of the stairs. The man standing there looks hard at your sister, then marks an X with chalk on her coat.

As you move forward a woman near you whispers, "Quick! Get your sister to turn her coat inside out!"

You nod and grab your sister. You pull off her coat and turn it inside out so the chalk mark doesn't show.

"Put it back on!" you tell her. She slips her arms back into the sleeves. It doesn't look too bad. Maybe no one will notice she is wearing it the wrong way out. You find out later, the chalk mark meant she was thought to have a mental illness. She would have been put in another room to be examined by doctors. They might have kept her on Ellis Island or even sent her back to Ireland.

But because the chalk mark is hidden, that doesn't happen. In just a few hours, you are registered and free to enter the country! A boat takes you back to New York City, where your aunt and uncle are waiting. As the boat docks, you take one last look at the lady with the torch, standing tall in the harbor.

Ever since 1886, the Statue of Liberty has welcomed new arrivals to New York. Back then she greeted boat passengers. Today airplane passengers peer out the windows, trying to get a glimpse of this famous lady. The statue was a gift from France to the United States as a symbol of freedom and friendship between the two countries. Gustave Eiffel, who designed the Eiffel Tower in France, helped create the statue. She was constructed in Paris and then taken apart into 350 pieces to be shipped across the Atlantic to New York.

Lady Liberty is made of a thin copper "skin" supported by a web of steel bars. The copper is only about the thickness of two pennies. It turned green as it weathered. If you want to get an idea of the statue's size, think of your own height. Liberty's nose is four feet, six inches tall (1.48 m). Is Liberty's nose taller or shorter than you?

Liberty stood as a beacon of hope to the millions of immigrants who came through the harbor on their way into the country. The full name of the statue was "Liberty Enlightening the World". Poetess Emma Lazarus expressed the feelings of these newcomers about the statue:

> *Give me your tired, your poor,*
> *Your huddled masses yearning to breathe free,*
> *The wretched refuse of your teeming shore;*
> *Send these, the homeless, tempest-tost to me,*
> *I lift my lamp beside the golden door!**

Jesus makes this offer too. "Come to me," he says, "all of you who are weary and carry heavy burdens, and I will give you rest" (Matthew 11:28). Anyone who comes to Jesus finds true freedom. Freedom from having to do what's wrong – and freedom to begin living God's way. Jesus said about himself: "I am the light of the world. If you follow me, you won't be stumbling through the darkness, because you will have the light that leads to life" (John 8:12).

Sometimes you might feel like you are stumbling in the dark, when things go wrong or you don't know what to do next. You can talk to Jesus about it – he will help you to think clearly about a problem. Ask someone who follows Jesus to help you find answers in the Bible. He wants to guide us every day, so that we can live in his light.

The new arrivals had left their home countries for many reasons. Perhaps their crops had failed and work was scarce. Others were not allowed to believe what they wanted. They saw

---

*From the poem *The New Colossus* by Emma Lazarus, 1883. The complete poem is written on a tablet inside the Statue of Liberty pedestal.

America as a land where they could find work and be free to worship as they wanted to. Ellis Island became the gateway to America, and over the years twelve million immigrants were processed here.

The so-called "six second doctors" who watched immigrants climb the staircase had to decide if they were fit to enter the country. Did they have mental problems? Something wrong with the feet? A heart problem? Imagine trying to discover a medical problem, based on looking quickly at someone who was wearing several layers of clothing! They used seventeen different chalk symbols, each pointing to a possible illness or defect. Anyone with a chalk mark would be pulled aside and examined more carefully.

If you passed the medical inspection, you were allowed to enter the vast Great Hall where immigrants were registered. You probably weren't noticing the beautiful arched ceiling. You sat jammed together with hundreds of others on rows of wooden benches, waiting your turn to go up to the inspection desks. It was horribly hot and stuffy. People near you were jabbering in all kinds of languages you had never heard before. The stink of unwashed bodies was overpowering.

When your turn finally came, an inspector would check your name on the list of passengers from your steamship. If you were a man, he would ask you some questions. Are you married? How much money do you have? What is your occupation? Have you ever been convicted of a crime?

For women it was even harder. They had to answer all the questions, but even if they passed, they could not enter on their own. A husband or guardian had to come for them. Weddings occasionally took place on Ellis Island, so that a woman could enter America.

THINGS TO SEE AND DO

- Ellis Island.
- The Statue of Liberty.
- Allow a half-day for each, and book ahead online to avoid long lines for the ferry. If you can only visit one, you will pass very close to the statue on the way to Ellis Island.

Today one of the most fascinating things to do in New York City is to take a tour of the Ellis Island immigration facility. The audio tour makes you feel you are really there, experiencing the life of an arriving passenger. Do you know if any of your ancestors came into this country through Ellis Island? You can search the passenger records online through the Ellis Island website.

The immigrants sailing past Liberty into New York Harbor were sure they had reached paradise on earth. Did the city live up to their hopes and dreams?

Streets Paved with Gold

"They say the streets of New York are paved with gold, is that true?"

"Then I'll take a hammer and chip some off, and we'll be rich!"

"Look – across the water – I see the city. It looks like heaven!"

You arrive in a steamship, packed in like pigs going to market. Your first view of New York harbor takes your breath away. The gigantic statue welcomes you and the city is ablaze with lights. Back home you had candles and oil lamps, but in New York many buildings are lit by Thomas Edison's "electric illuminating system". Your family can hardly wait to land in this glorious place.

Finally you arrive in the city. But where is the New York of your dreams?

The electric lights you saw from the harbor don't light up your neighborhood. Instead of being paved with gold, the streets are dark and strewn with trash. In fact you can hardly see the streets, they are so crowded with people. Shoppers shove past horsecarts and pushcarts piled with goods. Kids swarm around, trying not to get run over. Watch where you step! It looks like everyone throws their garbage into the street, and there's plenty of horse manure too.

This was the scene on the Lower East Side, where many of the poor arrivals ended up. They crowded into gloomy apartment buildings called "tenements", where a whole family with several children would live in three tiny rooms. Children had to sleep on a cot in the kitchen or on living room chairs pushed together to make beds. It was a dismal place, especially for families used to living in a small country village in Europe.

There were no indoor toilets for many years, just stinking outhouses in the backyards. At night it was either too hot or too cold to bother going outside, so residents used chamber pots in their rooms. The next morning they sometimes emptied the pots out the window.

Some tenement landlords offered the first two weeks' rent free. So families might stay in one place two weeks, and then move to a new place. Kids would come home from school to find their family had moved. Imagine having to ask the neighbors where your new home was! Where would children play on these crowded blocks? They had to make do with rooftops, streets, and filthy alleys.

The backs of the buildings were so close together that sunlight never touched the lower windows or backyards. What little light might have reached down into the yards was blocked with lines of wet laundry strung between the buildings. Today you can walk down these streets and admire beautiful iron fire escapes. They made a good place to sleep in hot weather. Unfortunately, the residents back then frequently had to use them to flee fires which swept through whole blocks.

By 1910, some areas of the Lower East Side had over 1,200 residents per block. With thousands living squashed together like this, many caught diseases such as tuberculosis. The rats in the neighborhood were as big as cats.

No, the streets were not paved with gold. The immigrants had traveled so far, only to find conditions worse off than back home. This was no paradise. But there is a paradise, and we can go there.

Jesus taught that his followers would go to heaven to be with him. While he was dying, one of the criminals hanging on a cross next to him believed in him. Jesus said to the man, "I assure you, today you will be with me in paradise" (Luke 23:43). That is a promise for us too. If you want to belong to Jesus with your whole heart, you don't have to worry or wonder what will happen to you after you die. You can be sure that you will go straight to be with him forever. That will be more amazing than we can possibly imagine.

Back then if you walked down a street of tenements in the Jewish quarter you would hear a strange humming noise. You would see people sitting in most of the open windows. You might wonder why so many had time to admire the view. Actually, the front room of a tenement apartment was the only room with windows – the only source of good light. Those sitting in the windows were sewing. The steady hum was the noise of their machines.

Many of the early immigrant families set up their own little sewing factories right in their apartment. The children would help too. A teenage girl was often given the task of fine hand stitching to finish off a garment, because her eyesight would be the best for close work. The brothers might be runners who would fetch ready-cut pieces of cloth from other factories in the neighborhood and bring them home to be sewn into dresses.

The mother would try to raise a family and cook for the workers in a windowless kitchen the size of a closet. Meanwhile,

in the same room, the presser worked over a hot iron, ironing sections of finished garments. The apartment was crowded and steamy, with no cross ventilation. As many as twelve people might be working in this home factory. No wonder they called it a "sweatshop"!

There are still a few sweatshops operating on the Lower East Side. Of course they are illegal, and are usually found out. But immigrants who arrive not knowing English can be tricked into working long hours sewing garments, for very little pay.

When early immigrants poured into the city, they tended to live in areas where others spoke their language and where they could buy food to make their ethnic dishes. For many years an area along the East River was called Klein Deutschland – Little Germany. It held the largest German-speaking community outside of Europe. Jewish settlers lived in Yiddish-speaking neighborhoods where they could buy kosher food.

Whether they were Italian, Irish, German or Chinese, all made their own part of the city as much like their home culture as possible. For many years Manhattan was like an island of small towns. Each neighborhood had its own sights and sounds and smells. No one worried about locking their doors. Everyone knew everyone else in the neighborhood, and they all looked out for each other. You could buy your groceries on credit at the local shop.

Today you will often find residents of a dozen different backgrounds living on one block. Still, there are areas of the city which are mostly Ukranian, Latino or Korean. If you walk through Little India, the smell of curry from Indian restaurants fills the air. On the Lower East Side you can find Jewish foods such as knishes, which are square pastries filled with meat or cheese or potato. Of all the original neighborhoods, Chinatown has kept more of its unique character. Even the street signs are in Chinese.

THINGS TO SEE AND DO

- Lower East Side Tenement Museum – a fascinating tour of life in real tenements. Book ahead online and allow a couple of hours – 108 Orchard Street.
- Chinatown.
- Eat at an Italian restaurant in Little Italy – Mulberry Street area.

There was only one place where newcomers from all backgrounds gathered together. In the late 19th and early 20th Centuries there were no radio, movies, TV or computers. Immigrants couldn't afford pricey theater or opera. What could the family do for fun? New York's Fourteenth Street Theater began offering wholesome variety shows called "vaudeville". A ticket cost only fifty cents.

Singers and dancers performed, but also escape artists, strong men, acrobats who wound their bodies into weird shapes, fire eaters, high divers and just about anything that could possibly be staged. People from all cultures laughed and clapped together in the popular vaudeville theaters.

Although vaudeville gave them something fun to do, most immigrants had a hard life. New Yorkers in the wealthy parts of the city didn't think much about what went on in the poor neighborhoods. That is, until a man with a flash camera showed them. We'll learn about him in the next chapter.

Think about it – if you were living in a cramped, smelly tenement apartment, would you be doomed to be miserable? How could you be happy, living like that?

You probably live in a much nicer place than the immigrants did. But there may be things other kids have that you don't. What do you do? Grumble and complain? Nag your parents? Do you think you'll really start living, once you get more things?

Jesus says he wants you to enjoy life now. He doesn't think you need more things in order to be happy. You might think you need a new toy or game or phone. You might wish for clothes just like your best friend has. You may want lots of other stuff, but Jesus knows what you really need and he promises to give you that. He wants you to make him and his kingdom the main things you focus on, and not worry about the rest (Matthew 6: 25-34). That's the sure way to be happy, no matter where you live or what you do or don't have.

In spite of the horrible conditions in the tenements, elsewhere in New York life was good. America had moved into the Gilded Age. The wealthy believed their riches would last forever. Do you think they were right?

Boom and Bust

"Come here Watson, I want you."

With these words Alexander Graham Bell called his assistant on a new apparatus – the telephone. Bell was one of the inventors of this device, which could convert the human voice into electrical impulses and back into something sounding like the voice.

Soon the first New York "phone book" appeared. Actually it was a card with the names of 252 residents who had telephones. You paid $20 a month for phone service. If you wanted to make a call, you'd pick up the phone and ask to be connected with someone on the list.

Then there was electric light. Thomas Edison didn't invent the light bulb, but he was the first one to make it practical. Thomas was a businessman as well as a clever designer of more than a thousand inventions. He made the first phonograph, which could record and play back sound. That seems very ordinary to us, but back then it was like magic.

He also experimented with something he called the Kinetograph. We would call it a motion picture camera. You could watch short films through a peephole viewer called a Kinetoscope. Eventually a way was found to project these to a whole room, and modern cinema was born. Early cinema was dangerous – the celluloid film was highly flammable. The bright light needed to project it could cause the film to burst into flame. Soon cinema houses were built, so that the projection box could be kept separate from the audience.

When Thomas was at school, he had trouble paying attention. His teacher referred to him as "addled". Today we might say "he's a dreamer". His mother decided to teach him at home after that. He said later, "She was so sure of me; and I felt I had something to live for, someone I must not disappoint." And he did not disappoint her. Out of his "dreaming" came ideas that touch each one of us today.

It's wonderful to have someone who inspires us, like Thomas Edison's mother did. Jesus can be that for us, if we let him. He knows what we can become because he made us! He also knows our weaknesses, but he loves us anyway. Jesus will help us be the best we can possibly be. Ask him each day to help you live in a way that brings joy to him.

The late 1800s in America became known as the Gilded Age. New inventions changed the way people lived, and the nation was thriving. Wealthy New Yorkers began moving north on Fifth Avenue, where they built ornate mansions. There are only a few of these left today.

The wealthy tried to outdo each other in showing off their money. In their homes they had private ballrooms and theaters and, of course, electric lights. Expensive works of art hung on the walls. In the afternoons they would be driven in carriages through Central Park, where they would show off their fine horses to their rich neighbors.

Mrs. Astor had a famous list of 400 people who she considered worthy of being invited to her home. Supposedly it was the number of guests who would fit in her ballroom. Of course all the rich wanted to be on that list. New York was becoming supreme in size and in every other way. It was the showcase of the Gilded Age.

An object is "gilded" when it is covered with a thin layer of gold. The gold is only on the outside. That was the case for the Gilded Age as well. When we look closer at what was happening then, we see greed and the desire to get rich quick. Not everyone enjoyed a good life. Other New Yorkers lived in tiny airless rooms. The two sides of the city rarely met each other. The rich hardly knew the poor existed, until Jacob Riis came along.

THINGS TO SEE AND DO

- Empire State Building – Fifth Avenue near East 34th Street – go as early as possible to avoid long lines.
- Metropolitan Museum – 1000 Fifth Avenue at Central Park – check out the Arms and Armor Hall and the Mummy Hall.

Jacob grew up in Denmark in a family with 15 children and moved to the U.S. in 1870. He was trained as a carpenter, but had trouble finding work and ended up homeless in a snowstorm with only a nickel in his pocket. The best he could do was to sleep in dreary police station lodging houses.

He finally got a job as a reporter for a weekly newspaper. During this time he attended a church revival meeting and trusted his life to Jesus. His new faith gave him a soft heart for the poor. He decided to use the paper as a way to let New Yorkers know what life was like in the hidden parts of the city.

Jacob would walk down the most dangerous streets of the city late at night, carrying a camera and tripod but also wearing a gun strapped to his coat. He would talk to people and get them to agree to be photographed. He was even allowed inside the dark, crowded apartments to take pictures. Some of the people he photographed were members of gangs. As soon as the bright flash went off, Jacob would escape as quickly as he could before any trouble started.

He was one of the first in America to use the newly invented flash powder for photography. This flared up in an instant, so that the people were captured by the camera before they had time to react. Still, he was once chased by a mob of angry women, who threw stones and yelled at him to stay out of their neighborhood.

Jacob eventually brought out a book, *How the Other Half Lives*. Because he used a flash, people saw for the first time what life inside the dark tenements was like. After reading the book, the police commissioner closed down the horrible police lodging houses. The commissioner was Theodore Roosevelt, who later became president of the United States as well as a friend of Jacob.

For many years Jacob gave lectures and showed projection slides of his pictures. Women wearing fine dresses were horrified as they understood for the first time, how the workers who made their clothing actually lived. Jacob would end his talks by encouraging his listeners to follow Jesus. He knew that Jesus loved and cared for the poor. That's what he was hoping New Yorkers would do, too.

As a result of his work, some of the worst tenements were torn down to make parks. Playgrounds were added to vacant lots. New Yorkers began to care about the poor of their city. Eventually in 1934, Mayor Fiorello LaGuardia created the New York Housing Authority. We'll learn more in the last chapter about how New York helps its poor and homeless today.

Everyone thought the Gilded Age would go on forever. The 1920s were known as the "Roaring Twenties". In 1928 the new president Herbert Hoover said, "We in America today are nearer to the final triumph over poverty than ever before in the history of any land."

Then in September of 1929, the New York stock market "crashed". Millions of Americans owned shares in various companies, but suddenly everyone wanted to sell out. Traders at the Wall Street exchange shouted and screamed as major companies began to lose all their money.

After the Wall Street crash came the era known as the Great Depression which affected all parts of society, including the wealthy. Many lost their jobs and homes. Some who had made their fortunes were out on the street, looking for work. But everyone else needed work too. There were too many workers and not enough jobs.

If you were out on the street, where would you go? One family moved into a cave in Central Park and stayed there for a year.

In the rest of the country things were just as bad. Farmers couldn't get enough money for their wheat or corn, so they left crops to rot in the fields. Parents didn't have money to buy new school shoes for their kids. When the old ones wore out, they stuffed them with cardboard. The homeless took refuge in shacks made from scrap metal and boxes. Thousands of children were among them. Songs like "Brother, can you spare a dime?" expressed how Americans felt as they sank into poverty.

In spite of the Depression, construction began in 1930 on one of New York's most famous sights. The Empire State Building on the corner of Fifth Avenue and 34th Street has 102 stories, plus a 200-foot tower. It was the tallest building in the city for forty years.

When it opened in 1931, nobody could afford to rent space there. It was nicknamed the "Empty State Building".

But the observatories became popular places to go. You can still visit the 86th floor today for fantastic views of New York. It has to be closed in storms, though, because the tower acts like a giant lightning conductor. The building gets hit by lightning about 100 times a year.

This observatory is a favorite place for filmmakers, and scenes from movies such as *Sleepless in Seattle* have been shot here. It's also a popular spot for romance. However, there is a lot of static electricity on top of the building. Kissing couples may feel their lips crackling with sparks!

If you visit New York, you'll notice that the Empire State Building is lit up at night. You may be imagining a boring white light, but you'll be surprised at the colors. Every few days the colors change, to honor particular groups or events. For example, the building turns green for St. Patrick's Day, and red, white and blue for the Fourth of July. When a baseball team wins a series, it lights up with the colors of the winning team.

On foggy nights during the bird migration season, the building is not lit up as usual. This is to protect the flocks of birds, which are attracted to this huge column of light and would be killed flying into it.

In addition to the colored lights, there are revolving electronic beacons on the base of the tower which can be seen from 300 miles away by air. On top of the tower is a flashing red beacon light which warns aircraft to stay clear.

Sometimes the bulb inside this important red beacon has to be changed. If the light goes dark, a plane might fly into it. How would you like to be the one to change that bulb? It's a scary but vital task. The man who does it these days is a trained electrical engineer and climber. Fortunately it only has to be changed about every five years.

Did you know you are a beacon? Jesus told his followers that he was the light of the world. But he said that they were lights too. He compared them to a city on top of a mountain, glowing in the dark for all to see (Matthew 5:15). If he visited New York City today, he might say that his followers are like the beacons on the Empire State Building. Their lives should shine out to everyone around them.

But what if the bulb grows dim, or fades out? How do we keep our "beacon" bright and strong?

One of the best ways is through prayer.

Prayer is simply talking with God. You can let him know how you are feeling about the way things are going. Of course he already knows, but when we pray, we feel closer to him. We sense his encouragement. Don't forget to pray for others, too. God wants us to be part of what he's doing in the world. When we pray, he acts. Things may not change right away, but you can be sure that God is working behind the scenes, if you are praying.

He can work without us, but he wants us to share in the fun of seeing him answer.

Come along now as we head to the north of the city, to visit a neighborhood that felt the boom of the Roaring Twenties more than any other.

Hopping in Harlem

The scene is a small apartment in New York City. All the furniture has been pushed out of the way. There's a man playing the piano, another with a sax and someone on drums. The whole neighborhood is throbbing to the beat of their jazz. The apartment fills up with guests, and the smell of fried food makes your mouth water. Then everyone starts dancing the Lindy Hop. Couples look like acrobats in the circus as the men throw their partners over their heads. It's a typical Saturday night "rent party" in 1920s Harlem.

Before the Harlem Railroad was built, the only way to reach this distant suburb of the city was by steamboat or a large stagecoach called an "omnibus". Then in the early 1830s tracks were laid for trams, which were still drawn by horses.

Horse trams were faster and gave a smoother ride than stagecoaches, but horses weren't ideal for city transport. Can you think why? For one thing, the animals could only work for about five hours a day. They had to be fed and cared for and stabled. And of course, they produced lots of manure! The streetcar company had to shovel it off the streets and figure out what to do with it.

Once the railroad was built, it was easy to reach Harlem, which is north of Central Park. The area became a pleasant middle-class suburb filled with rows of houses known as "brownstones". In the 1800s these narrow, deep homes were built all over the city, from local brown sandstone. Brownstones usually had steps leading up to the main door and another entrance to the ground floor, where servants would live. Many of these houses can still be seen in Harlem today.

Can you imagine having laws that keep people separate, according to the color of their skin? That's what some southern states did, after the Civil War. Special laws were put in force to say blacks had to live separately from whites. They could not sit in the same bus waiting room. They had to use separate drinking fountains. Restaurants had to have separate dining rooms for black and white customers. Many blacks moved north to New York City to escape such laws.

The reason behind these laws was the idea that whites were somehow better than blacks. I'm sure you think it's wrong, that a whole group of people could be looked down on, just because of their skin color. Yet it was a way of life for supposedly "free" blacks living in the south for a hundred years. These unjust laws lasted into the 1960s.

It's hard to understand how this can happen, but it does. We can be afraid of people who are different from us. We may try to avoid them. This is not God's idea! When God came to earth, he came as a Middle Eastern baby. He spent time as a refugee in Africa. Jews in the city of Jerusalem looked down on Jesus because he was from the country. He knew what it was like to be treated with scorn.

The Bible tells us that God gave his son Jesus for every person on the planet. So God values each of us very highly, no matter what color we are. If that's true, how does he want us to treat those who are different from us? Think about someone at your school, who everyone avoids or teases. Maybe someone who looks different from the other kids, or who doesn't do well in their school work. Or it might be someone who has come from another country. How can you be a friend to that person?

Blacks moved to New York looking for better jobs and better schools for their children. Many bought homes in Harlem for the first time. There was still racial prejudice in the city, but not the laws which completely separated black and white. So most were better off than in the south.

Harlem began to attract black writers, artists and musicians. They felt they could do good creative work there. Writers would gather in each other's homes and read out their plays or poetry. Suddenly a whole group of African-Americans living in one place were proud of their culture. This sparked what is known as the Harlem Renaissance of the 1920s.

THINGS TO SEE AND DO
- Sylvia's Restaurant – 328 Lenox Avenue.
- Apollo Theater – 253 West 125th Street.
- Dwyer Cultural Center – St. Nicholas Avenue at 123rd Street.

Renaissance simply means rebirth. This was also a time when something else was born: jazz music. Jazz grew out of ragtime music with African-American blues added, in unpredictable ways. Although it was invented mostly in New Orleans, Harlem musicians like Duke Ellington and Fats Waller helped make it popular. Clubs in Harlem played this new music, and people from the south part of New York flocked north to experience it.

Harlem poet Langston Hughes wrote about this sudden popularity of the African-American culture. Everyone wanted to visit Harlem. Whites wanted to sing and dance to black music. For the first time there was a play on Broadway with an all-black cast. Whites even went to Harlem churches to watch the enthusiastic way blacks worshipped. Sometimes black people felt like animals in a zoo.

One way to escape this was through "rent parties". A card advertising a "Social Whist Party" or "Tea Cup Party" would appear in the hall of an apartment building. But these words were like a secret code. For a small fee you could turn up on a Saturday night at someone's apartment for music and dancing and refreshments. Sometimes a big jazz star would show up and play the piano, just for fun. At rent parties, Harlem residents could get together without outsiders watching them.

Then came the Wall Street Crash of 1929, followed by the Great Depression. Just as in the whole of America, many in Harlem lost their jobs and their homes. Harlem was no longer the popular place to go.

The Harlem Renaissance had seemed like a miracle. Its effects spread far and wide, as jazz took hold and swept the country and the world. This new music lifted the spirits of Americans who were stuck in the Depression. African-Americans were encouraged by all that had been achieved by the creative minds of Harlem.

But for the neighborhood itself, the renaissance didn't last. It turned into a run-down dangerous area which it was best to avoid. For decades, many of Harlem's residents lived without even heat or hot water in their apartments.

In 1986 a group of Harlem churches got together and prayed. Then they formed an organisation to tackle problems such as poverty, poor housing and health care. They realised Harlem needed more than just a little help – it needed a resurrection. Partly through the help of churches like these, Harlem has slowly turned the corner. Today it is a safer place which is attracting people to move in from other parts of the city.

What is there to see in Harlem today? You can visit the famous Apollo Theater on 125th Street, where singers like Ella Fitzgerald were discovered. They still have talent nights on Wednesdays, where anyone who wants can turn up and try to impress the audience. However if they don't like you, be prepared to be booed offstage! The Jackson Five won an amateur night here in 1967.

And there's Sylvia's Restaurant which offers Southern cooking and live gospel music on Sundays. Bethel Gospel Assembly, which features in the last chapter of this book, is located there. The new Dwyer Cultural Center provides exhibits and events which celebrate Harlem's history and creativity. Harlem has had a slow and steady resurrection, as a result of much prayer and hard work.

Another kind of resurrection took place in the Bible – one that was sudden and unexpected. After Jesus died his followers were heartbroken. They had spent three years with him and they were really close friends. They couldn't understand how God could let this happen.

But three days later, some of his friends said they'd seen him. Others didn't believe it. One day they were meeting in a closed room when Jesus appeared out of nowhere! God had brought him back to life.

Jesus didn't come back in the same body. It was a special kind of body that would never die again. His new body could travel wherever he wanted in an instant. He could suddenly appear in a room, and then disappear.

The resurrection of Jesus was very important. It showed that God has the power over death and evil. We don't see God's power fully today, and it sometimes seems like evil gets the upper hand in the world. The world may look like it's falling apart, but God has big plans to renew it. And he wants you to be a part of making that happen! When you live as his follower, then others will begin to see that God is real.

One day, all of creation will know God as their king. But for now, there is a lot of work to do in places like Harlem.

In the next chapter, we'll discover some of New York's wildlife – but it's not the kind you see in the countryside.

Forty Thieves and Egyptian Dragons

As sly as coyotes, as common as bedbugs and more dangerous than hawks searching for prey – what creatures are these? They were not found out in nature but prowling the streets of New York. They had names like Forty Thieves, Plug Uglies, Bowery Boys, Dead Rabbits. Many times in New York's history, violent gangs like these have terrorized parts of the city.

One of the worst gang areas in the 19th Century was known as Five Points, where five streets came together. It was an overcrowded slum filled with disease. Wild West hero Davy Crockett visited the neighborhood and said he'd rather go into Indian country than go back there! It no longer exists, but was near the present location of Columbus Park.

The main goal of a number of gangs was to rob and steal. Pickpockets were common and there was even a criminal called Dopey Benny who ran a school for pickpockets, just like Fagin in *Oliver*. Each gang had its own few blocks where they ruled like tyrants. Some of them were so dangerous, the police wouldn't dare to go into their territory.

Other gangs were simply groups of teenagers, protecting themselves and their friends as they walked to school. They would wear the same kind of clothes and stick closely together. You knew which streets belonged to which gangs, and you'd be in danger if you wandered into the wrong street.

Many of these gangs grew out of conditions on the crowded, desperately poor Lower East Side. With so many squashed in airless tenements, it's no wonder crime was a problem. When you lived in such close quarters, it was only natural you'd want to stay out on the streets as much as possible. Gangs provided a group to hang out with. In a way, they were like family.

Although gang families caused trouble, God invented families. He knows we need a group to belong to, who accept us just the way we are and stick up for us no matter what. We don't always have human families like that, although it's wonderful when we do. But God says his family is a loving one. When we become Jesus' followers, we instantly become members of God's family – people all over the world who love God and want to live for him. God is our father and Jesus is like our older brother. They will love us no matter what.

What do you think God's family is like? In looks, we can be anything: young, old, rich, poor, every shape and size and color. What about our actions and attitudes? Can you think of ways that God's children might stand out from the crowd?

Gang members wanted to stand out too, but in all the wrong ways. Partly due to the gangs, New York was a crime-infested place for many years. Even the police and politicians had a bad reputation. People felt like giving up on the city. What can we do when evil seems to take the upper hand? Either we give up, or we work on, doing what we can. "Don't let evil get the best of you," we read in the Bible, "but conquer evil by doing good" (Romans 12:21).

That has been the experience of pastor David Wilkerson. He had no idea that just flicking through the pages of a magazine would change his life – and the lives of many others.

It happened in 1958, at a time when New York gangs were again on the rise. David was minister of a church in a small town in the mountains of Pennsylvania, hundreds of miles from New York City. He was in the habit of watching television late at night after his work was done. One night after he turned off the TV, it crossed his mind that the program he'd just watched was pointless. He decided to sell the TV and spend that time in prayer instead.

One night during his prayer time, his eyes were drawn to a magazine on his desk. He began flicking through the magazine, when he caught sight of a drawing of seven gang members on trial for murder. These were New York teenagers, members of a violent gang called the Egyptian Dragons. Something about the eyes of these young killers touched the pastor. He sensed God speaking to him: "Go to New York and help these boys."

At first he tried to ignore it. He didn't know anything about gangs in New York, and he didn't want to! He and his family were happy where they were. But he couldn't get the thought out of his mind. God wanted him to go to New York. He had to go.

So a few days later David got in his car and drove to New York City. He arrived at the courtroom, full of faith that God was going to use him somehow with these seven young killers. But that didn't happen. After the day's session he was trying to speak to the judge, when he was grabbed by guards and thrown outside. Flashbulbs went off in his face. His picture appeared in newspapers under the headline, "Bible-waving Preacher Interrupts Trial."

How embarrassing! The people at his church back home felt sorry for him. He felt like a failure. But he couldn't shake off the idea that God wanted him to reach teen gangs in New York. So he went back. He'd only been on the street a few minutes when some young gang members called him by name. "Aren't you the preacher they kicked out of the trial?" one of them asked. They had seen his picture in the newspaper. "You're one of us," they said.

This puzzled David. But the gang members explained that the cops didn't like him, and they didn't like the gangs either. That made David a safe person for them to talk to. Within an hour, the pastor found himself in a basement gang hideout. He told the group of teens that God loved them just the way they were, but that he had better hopes for them than the way they were living.

"You're coming through," one boy said. He meant, you're reaching our hearts.

David spent hours with these young gang members. Many were hooked on drugs and alcohol. He helped them see that only Jesus was able to free them and make them new. As they put themselves into God's hands, many had their lives changed completely.

One of the most famous of these was a young man named Nicky Cruz. Nicky was one of 18 children of Puerto Rican parents. His parents practiced witchcraft. Even as a young child,

Nicky was severely mistreated by them. He grew up tough – nobody could reach his heart. By age 16 he was one of the leaders of the Brooklyn gang known as the Mau Maus. Even the police were afraid of this violent gang.

Newspapers called Nicky "The Garbage-Can Fighter." He had a metal garbage can with a hole cut in one side to see out of. In a fight he would stick the can over his head for protection and start swinging his baseball bat. Everyone thought he was a hopeless case.

Even David Wilkerson thought that, when he first met Nicky. He tried to reach out to him, saying that he loved him. Nicky reacted with, "If you come near me, Preacher, I'll kill you!" But the pastor just kept on praying and showing Nicky that Jesus loved him.

The love of Jesus and the message of forgiveness finally melted Nicky's heart. At a meeting where Pastor David preached, Nicky went forward. He knelt down and prayed for the first time in his life. "Dear God," he said, "I'm the dirtiest sinner in New York. I don't think you want me. If you do want me, you can have me. As bad as I was before, I want to be that good for Jesus."

Pastor David didn't know if Nicky was really praying that night, or if it was a joke to this hardened youth. But the next time he saw Nicky, he saw a different person. Instead of a hard, sullen face, the pastor saw a smiling young man whose eyes were lit up. He told David he wanted to be a preacher – to bring light into the darkness of the gang world.*

And that's what he started to do. Nicky told gang members that Jesus could change their lives, and they believed him. They

---

* The story of how David came to New York and how Nicky came to faith is told in the book *The Cross and The Switchblade*, by the Reverend David Wilkerson, with John and Elizabeth Sherrill.

knew what he was like before, and they saw what Jesus was making him into. Here was a young man who had traded his baseball bat for a Bible. He was clean from drugs. He was filled with the joy of knowing he was completely forgiven.

For the past fifty years, Nicky Cruz has traveled all over the world, telling the hopeless there is hope for them with God's love. He especially speaks in cities where youth are trapped in drugs, violence and gangs. On his website is this question:

"What would happen if instead of cursing the darkness we invaded it with light?"

While New York's gangs have tried their best to rob and destroy, God has raised up others to help. David Wilkerson realized the gangs wore certain clothes and hats and sunglasses to try and hide how scared and lonely they were. He stepped out in faith, not having any idea where his trip to New York would lead. Eventually he moved his family to New York and founded an organization called Teen Challenge.

Today Teen Challenge centers around the world take in young people who are gang members or hooked on drugs and alcohol. These troubled youths live with Christians who show them every day how much Jesus loves them. They learn to deal with their main problem – sin. As mentioned earlier in this book, that's the word the Bible uses to describe going our own way, doing what we please and not giving God a thought. Not only the Teen Challenge residents but each one of us has a sin problem. We tend to ignore God and try to make it on our own. We may try our best to change, but without his help, we can't. We need Jesus to come inside us and change us from the inside out.

The way he does that is by his Spirit. You can't see the Holy Spirit, because he's like the wind. You can't see the wind, but you can feel it on your face or see the trees move when it blows. And you can see where the Spirit of Jesus is moving, by watching how he changes lives. Jesus said that he was the only one who could really set us free from our sin (John 8:36). He does that by means of his Spirit living inside us.

When the Teen Challenge youth come to Jesus, he gives them a complete makeover from the inside out. They no longer want to go on with their old messed-up lives. They want to live for him. Some of them stay on at the centers and become workers who help others to get free from their harmful habits. They come alongside those who are lost and desperate, helping them in their new faith.

If you have given your life to Jesus, you also need others to come alongside you. Don't try to be a Christian on your own. Find a church where Jesus is loved and spoken about, and where the Bible is taught. Make sure it's a place where there are programs for young people. We need the encouragement of those who have followed Jesus for a while and can help show us the way. It's wonderful being part of God's big family.

In 1987 David Wilkerson started Times Square Church, set in the very heart of the city. This is near the spot where, each December 31, the square is packed with people celebrating the New Year. The church calls this place "the crossroads of the world." They draw visitors from around the globe as they reach

---

THINGS TO SEE AND DO

- Times Square – Seventh Avenue and Broadway.
- Times Square Church – 237 West 51st at Broadway.
- FAO Swartz – the most famous toy store in the world – Fifth Avenue at 58th Street.
- Top of the Rock observatory at Rockefeller Center – 50th Street between Fifth and Sixth Avenue.

---

out to the needy of New York and beyond, with practical aid and the message of Jesus.

Today there are still gangs in New York, but not so many. One reason is that the neighborhoods today are mostly mixed, made up of residents from many backgrounds. And the gangs are mixed too. Also, the New York Police Department now has a Gang Division of 300 officers. When they get word of a gang fight, they can respond quickly to break it up. Gangs can only operate on the street, but they find it harder when the police keep showing up.

In the next chapter, let's take a break from the streets of New York and head for nature to find some real wildlife.

Wild in the City

You stand on a massive rock overlooking a calm lake. Large trees cast green reflections in the water. In the distance a white egret takes flight, soaring overhead and finally landing on a small island in the lake. The sky is gray and there's no one else around. A nearby sign warns that this is a "Quiet Area" – no music or phones allowed.

Where are you? You might think you're in rural New York State, but in fact you're in the very heart of the city. Or rather, the lungs. This is Turtle Pond in Central Park, the green oasis that gives residents a break from the smells and sounds of the city canyons. Central Park is how the city breathes.

Built between 1857 and 1860, it was the first landscaped city park in America. Most of the city's residents lived crowded together below 38th Street. The few who lived in the area where Central Park is now (between 59th Street and 110th Street) were mostly ragpickers who sifted through garbage to find things to sell. The land itself was swampy. Workers had to blast out rocks and move tons of earth to sculpt the park. Topsoil was brought in from New Jersey. Walls had to be built to protect the 270,000 new plants from the pigs and goats which wandered the area.

As soon as the frozen Central Park lake was open to the public in the winter of 1858, it was filled with ice skaters. This tradition of skating in Central Park has continued ever since, although now it's allowed only on the artificial rink near the southern end of the park.

During the early years, the wealthy would dress up and ride in carriages through this new landscaped area and attend Saturday concerts here. It was too far for many poor people to come, and anyway they worked every day except Sunday. So Central Park with its rolling open countryside was mostly for the rich. That changed over the years. In the 20th Century playgrounds were added and rules were relaxed to allow ball games and walking on the grass. Finally it became a park for everyone, as it is today.

Maybe you'd like to visit Central Park Zoo to see the penguins, sea lions and polar bears being fed. There are still plenty of other animals too – they haven't all headed off to Madagascar! Birds fly right past your head in the rainforest building.

If you want to bring a picnic, then find a nice grassy spot on one of the many meadows. You can climb on the Alice in Wonderland Statue near the Conservatory Water. Head for the Belvedere Castle for great views over the park, and you'll find a small wildlife exhibit there. Or maybe you just want to enjoy the cool green spaces of this beauty spot.

As the trees have grown over the years, each section of the park now has a secluded feeling. But that only adds to the sense of escaping from the throbbing city. The 26,000 trees here have a big job to do. While buses and cars pump out carbon dioxide, trees soak it up. Then they breathe out fresh oxygen. Their leaves help buffer noise and their roots keep the land from eroding.

They not only protect the environment, they are good for the soul. After a hectic day of walking up and down the city, just step into the park. Ahh. Now you can relax.

Did you know you can be like a tree? The first Psalm, from the book of Psalms in the Bible says this. It describes people who filter out the bad stuff that comes from the world around us. These individuals don't follow the crowd and do what everyone else is doing. Instead, they listen to God's teachings and enjoy living the way God says. They are like trees planted along a riverbank, which soak up water and have healthy leaves and fruit.

One great way to know God's teachings is to read the Bible. If you have never read the Bible, why not try an experiment. Spend a few minutes each day reading from the gospel of Mark. This is an action-packed book which tells the story of Jesus' life. If you read half a chapter a day, it would take about a month to finish

the book. Try and find a modern translation of the Bible, such as the Living Bible, which will make it more clear. Ask God to speak to you through what you're reading. You will gradually understand more and begin to see changes in your life. Then you'll be as "green" as a tree in Central Park!

But the park is more than greenery. If you are there in the spring, watch out for babies – animal babies such as squirrels, rabbits, skunks, racoons and of course birds. What should you do if you run across one of these?

- Don't get too close, and don't try and take the baby home to care for it. The animal parents are the best caretakers. Just leave the baby alone and the parent will come back for it.

- Only move the baby if it's in danger of being run over, in which case you can put it behind a bush. Although you may have heard that animals or birds will reject the baby if they smell human scent on it, that is not true.

- If you see a baby hawk, owl or falcon on the ground, then call 311 and ask for the Urban Park Rangers. There is an army of well-trained park rangers who do everything from leading night hikes to helping you spot birds to rescuing animals. They will send someone who knows how to replace the bird in its nest.

- If a baby skunk or raccoon is making a loud noise, that's a sign it has been abandoned. You should call for a ranger and report the animal's exact location.

Another mammal you might run across in Central Park is the opossum. Like the kangaroo it is a marsupial, the only one in North America. The mother gives birth to tiny premature babies, as many as twenty-five at a time. They are born blind but manage to claw their way into a fur-lined pouch on her belly. For several weeks the babies stay in the pouch, feeding from the mother. When they are big enough to live outside, they ride on their mother's back while she hunts for food.

Occasionally you find a mammal where it's not supposed to be. Coyotes have been known to walk across a bridge into the city and end up in Central Park. One lady a couple of years ago encountered what she thought was a dog without a collar, but it turned out to be a coyote.

Soon police in flak jackets, reporters, photographers and park maintenance crew were all chasing the animal, which was nicknamed Hal. News helicopters hovered overhead, beaming the chase to the rest of the country. Finally the police got close enough to Hal to shoot him with a tranquilizer dart. Then they were able to cage him and take him away.

When you're on the lookout for mammals in the parks, don't forget to look up into the skies! Little brown bats look like birds, but they are mammals, the same as humans. They have hair instead of feathers and have teats from which they nurse their young. Baby bats can cling onto their mother and nurse even while she is flying.

A bat's skeleton looks a lot like yours, except for one thing – its fingers are almost as long as its body! The bat's "hands" are its wings. Bats roost in hollow trees and buildings during the day, and swarm out at dusk to feed on insects. Then they fly back to their homes just before the sun comes up. These little creatures do a great job cleaning up pests like mosquitoes.

In the spring, you can join birdwatchers as they look for the dozens of species that stop off in the city on their way north. These include many warblers, small songbirds with bright colorful plumage. Their short bills and wings make them very good at catching insects. One special treat for these little birds is provided by termite nests. When the termite larvae are old enough, they suddenly swarm out of the their nest. If you happen to be near a termite nest in Central Park when this happens, you'll see dozens of warblers swooping down and catching a flying snack.

The most famous bird of Central Park is a true New Yorker. He even has his own website! He has made his nest on the ledge of an apartment building at number 927 Fifth Avenue, overlooking the park. This is Pale Male, the brave red-tailed hawk who has become a local hero, attracting crowds with binoculars.

He and his mate, Lola. have raised more than twenty chicks with tourists and New Yorkers looking on.

The best place to see him is from the Conservatory Water where model boats are sailed. On the opposite side of this lake, photographer Rik Davis is often there to let visitors view the nest through a powerful telescope. If you are lucky enough to see the hawk couple, note that the female is larger than the male.

Central Park is only one of hundreds of parks and nature centers in New York, and it's not the largest. Freshkills Park on Staten Island won't open until 2030, but it promises to be extraordinary. At two-and-a-half times the size of Central Park, Freshkills used to be the largest garbage dump in the world! For fifty years, tons of household trash made its way each day from the city to Freshkills. There it was dumped onto mounds and then compacted many times by large bulldozers.

Eventually a mound would have so much garbage that it would be closed. Then it was covered with several feet of soil and topped by a waterproof membrane. Above this, several feet of clean soil and grasses were added to prevent erosion. The lower layer of soil contains a system for collecting the methane gas given off by the rotting garbage underneath. This gas is purified and used to heat 10,000 homes on Staten Island. Because the membrane is waterproof, rainwater runs off into catch ponds, which have become home to dragonflies, frogs, muskrats, fish and birds.

Just as Central Park was created out of an ugly site, Freshkills

THINGS TO SEE AND DO
- Watch animals being fed at the Central Park Zoo.
- American Museum of Natural History – Central Park West at 79th Street.
- Cosmic Collisions at the Hayden Planetarium – behind the American Museum of Natural History, shows every half hour.

Park is designed to be a place of beauty that everyone can enjoy. Already deer, raccoons and opossums and many unique wild birds have moved into the Freshkills site. Park rangers offer free guided tours of the area in a mini-van, but you need to book ahead.

New York City is surprisingly full of wildlife. But there is one kind of wildlife I hope you don't encounter there.

Have you ever heard someone say, "Goodnight, sleep tight, don't let the bedbugs bite"?

New Yorkers have been saying that a lot in recent years. Bedbugs are a big problem in the city. The bedbug is tiny, no bigger than an apple seed, but it can make life miserable. This insect is happiest when it is sucking your blood! It thinks your shoulders and arms are especially tasty.

The little critter pierces your skin and begins sucking, changing from light brown to red as it fills up with your blood. You might wake up in the morning with red blotches, which you think are mosquito bites. But look carefully at your sheets and you may see a few of these annoying creatures scurrying away.

Can you imagine going for a whole year without food? Well, the bedbug can. It can't fly, but that doesn't bother it. And if it wants to take a trip, it will just hitch a ride on your clothing or in your suitcase. The female lays up to 500 eggs at a time. So when you get rid of one bedbug, 500 more may be ready to take its place!

There's now even a department at New York's City Hall which has been set up to deal with bedbugs. It's hard to get rid of them – you have to call in professional exterminators. They live in clean apartments just as gladly as in dirty ones. To prevent getting them, don't take home any furniture you find sitting out on the sidewalk. And, at the risk of sounding like your mother, clean up your room! The more junk you have lying around, the more little hiding places you give the bedbugs.

But let's move on to a more pleasant topic. New York is a great place to celebrate the seasons. In the fall, everyone is glad the hot sticky summer is over. You can enjoy walking in the parks where trees turn brilliant orange and yellow and red. Winters can be harsh with plenty of snow. After a heavy snowfall, rangers in some parks will loan you a sled and serve hot chocolate to warm you up.

In spring the tulips and cherry blossoms are a relief after the long winter months. Summer can be unpleasantly humid, but you're allowed to splash around in the fountains. You can take a rest from the heat on garden chairs set up right around Times Square. It's the season to enjoy street fairs or head to the beaches to cool off. If you live in a place where you see the changing seasons, don't forget to thank God who designed them in a wonderful way.

This is our amazing God, who did miracles when he created the universe. He does miracles today too, as we'll find out in the next chapter.

Miracle on the Hudson

The jet engines roared as the Airbus 320 took off from New York's LaGuardia Airport, headed for Charlotte, North Carolina. It was a normal Thursday afternoon in January and the flight was one of dozens taking off from New York airports that day.

As the plane circled over the city, suddenly there was a big bang and the plane shook. Both engines went out. The pilot sent a message: "We've had a double bird strike!" A flock of geese had been sucked into the engines. The pilot had only seconds to think what to do with a heavy jet carrying 150 passengers. Below him was New York City. Just to the west lay the Hudson River, looking like a gray landing strip.

Passengers began to pray out loud as the plane headed down. Some repeated the Lord's prayer. The pilot warned everybody to brace themselves, then he landed the plane – right on the waters of the Hudson.

Although the Hudson is normally full of small boats, incredibly none were on that stretch of the river at that moment. As soon as the plane landed, though, three ferries chugged alongside to help. Passengers from the plane stepped out and stood shoulder-to-shoulder on the wing, just as if they were waiting on a subway platform. They were waist deep in ice-cold water. Soon rescue boats swarmed around and a helicopter dropped rescue divers into the water.

The plane bobbed along in the river, taking in water but not sinking completely. Once everyone was safely rescued, the plane was towed down the river and tied up at a south Manhattan dock. No one was killed. There were hardly any injuries.

The news reported "a miracle on the Hudson." Workers who watched the whole thing from high-rise buildings along the river said the plane landed gently, just like it was touching down on tarmac. It really did seem like a miracle. Many passengers thanked God that he protected them through what could have been a tragedy.

Our God is a God of miracles. Even ordinary life is full of them. If you're not sure about that, just find a mirror and look at your eyes. The eye is a ball with a lens on one side, out of which you see. This is protected by a tough coating called the cornea. On the back of the eye is a light-sensitive area of rods and cones called the retina, which turns light rays into electrical signals. These are fed to your brain by the optic nerve.

The pupil or center part of the eye expands and contracts, depending on the amount of light coming in. Inside the eyeball is a watery stuff which is replaced every four hours, and your tears keep the outside clean. Above the eye are your eyelid to keep it moist and eyelashes which protect it from dust.

That is only one of the complex, beautifully designed parts of the human body. It's crazy to think that something so perfectly tuned would just happen by chance. Someone had to think of it. That someone is God. We take our eyesight for granted, but it is one of the spectacular miracles engineered by the God who designed us.

The day of the "miracle on the Hudson" could have ended in tragedy, but it didn't. There was another day which did end in tragedy, the darkest day in New York's history: September 11, 2001 known now as 9/11. Two terrorist planes crashed into the twin towers of the World Trade Center. By the end of that day, nearly 3000 had died in terrorist attacks. The two buildings which had been the tallest in the city, towering over the skyline, were reduced to rubble.

You may wonder why this is in a chapter about miracles. But

even in the darkest time God is there, doing miracles. You may not see him at the time, but he is. We don't have any idea what all these miracles were, but consider a few. First of all, many office workers were able to escape before the towers fell. Also, the towers collapsed straight down. If the towers had fallen over, they would have hit a wide area. The death toll would have been nearer 50,000.

Another miracle was the timing. In fire stations all around the city, the day shift had just come to work while the night shift was getting ready to leave and go home. So stations had extra firemen on hand to help when the call came.

Other miracles took place when, instead of running away,

many people headed into the scene to help. Pastor Richard Del Rio was eating breakfast when he heard the towers had been attacked. He dropped his toast, grabbed his pastor's collar and police ID tag and ran out to his Harley-Davidson. It took him only minutes to reach the scene on his motorcycle. He was able to help get people in nearby shops to safety.

And everywhere he went, people saw his collar and asked him to pray. For a week he lived on just a few hours sleep a night, so that he could be on site to comfort rescue workers and pray with them. Through this pastor and others like him, many dazed and injured people had the experience of God being right there with them in this horrible time.

Where is God when trouble hits your life? He's in front of you, behind you and right beside you. If you have put your trust in Jesus, his Spirit is also in you. You can't get away from him, even if you don't feel him. You may be upset and worried, but let your mind focus on what you know is true – that God loves you and cares for you. He wants you to draw close to him in tough times.

When something bad happens, some turn away from God and blame him. Others turn to him for help. Which way do you think works best? What are some good things that might happen if you ask God for help when things go wrong? Is there something you want to talk to him about right now?

At this moment there are twenty-four massive cranes working on the construction site known as "Ground Zero." Buildings are starting to take shape. But the area where the two towers stood will be left like footprints, a memorial to those who died. We will be able to remember the tragedy, but also the miracles that took place here.

As we think over painful events such as the 9/11 disaster, we need to be able to forgive those who caused it. People who lost loved ones that day must have found this very hard.

Perhaps you have not experienced a huge terrible event like

THINGS TO SEE AND DO

- Overlook construction site of Ground Zero from the World Financial Center –220 Vesey Street.
- Battery Park on the southern tip of the island – views over the water to the Statue of Liberty.
- Catch the free Staten Island ferry from Battery Park for a round trip of all the harbor sights.

this, but in all of our lives things happen that we need to forgive. When someone hurts us, whether it's on purpose or accidentally, the natural reaction is to get angry. The Bible teaches that getting angry is not wrong – that's only human. The problem is if we decide to stay angry. That leads to a bitter attitude which is like a poison in our hearts. We want to pay the other person back. Pretty soon that's all we can think about. Our heart is so full of hatred and bad feelings, that after a while there is hardly any room for God.

If this has happened to you, the first thing to do is to ask God to forgive you. If you have told Jesus you believe in him and want to be his follower, you can be sure he has forgiven you for every wrong thing you have ever done. Yet you may find yourself still doing and thinking things you know don't make him happy. He's got rid of your big bag of "garbage," but you still collect little bits of trash as you go through your day. That's something we all do.

The Bible says if we admit our wrongs to Jesus, he is faithful to forgive us and keep us clean in his sight (1 John 1:9). It's a good idea to do this as soon as you become aware of anything wrong in your life. Then ask him to help you change. That's the way to stay close to him every day.

After you have asked forgiveness for yourself, ask God's help in forgiving others. This doesn't usually happen in an instant. You may need to keep on praying about it, until you know you are not holding a grudge any more.

In the last chapter we will visit a very special bridge, and meet some of God's hard-working secret agents in New York City.

Building Bridges to the World

In the winter of 1866, the East River froze over – again. As so often happened in winter, people who lived in Brooklyn had no easy way to get across to Manhattan Island. Normally they would take a ferry across, but with the river frozen the only way to get across was to walk on the ice.

Finally the city agreed it was time for a bridge. And what a bridge it turned out to be! The Brooklyn Bridge took thirteen years to build. The longest suspension bridge in the world, it was the first to be built with steel cables instead of iron. Its two towers were the tallest structures in the Western Hemisphere at that time. Over 125 years later it still spans the East River and is one of the most beautiful and famous bridges in the world.

Building the bridge was no easy matter. The original engineer John Roebling was badly injured before work even started, and died soon after. His son, Warren, took over, but he was paralyzed as a result of going underwater in a compression chamber.

These bottomless airtight shafts called "caissons" allowed workers to be under water to clear away silt and rocks, in order to lay the foundations for the two bridge towers. Compressed air was pumped in, to keep water from rising in the chambers. The men stood with their feet in freezing water while they dug into the mud of the riverbed. The mud and rocks they dug up were hoisted back up to the surface.

Workers were only able to stand the air pressure in the chamber for two hours before going back up. But if they went up too quickly they would get what they called "caisson sickness." This is what we call "the bends," a disease that can affect deep-sea divers. It can cause many symptoms including severe pain in the arms and legs, and even paralysis.

After Warren Roebling was paralyzed, his young wife, Emily, took over. This was at a time when women did not study engineering and weren't even allowed to vote. Emily learned the mathematical principles and terms needed to carry out the work. While her husband stayed in bed and advised her, she went back and forth to deal with the builders until the bridge was finished. She was the first person to ride across when the new bridge opened.

John Roebling had designed the Brooklyn Bridge to be six times as strong as he thought it needed to be. That may be the reason it's still standing, long after many other bridges built so long ago have crumbled. One surprising thing is that the tower on the Manhattan side doesn't rest on bedrock, as the Brooklyn tower does. The caisson workers were never able to dig down far enough to reach the bedrock on that side, so it rests on deep sand.

For the Brooklyn Bridge, this hasn't mattered. Roebling's design has proven to be sturdy enough. Most of the time though, building on sand is a bad idea. Jesus spoke about this, as he encouraged his listeners to obey what he said. Some people listen to Jesus' teachings and think, "That's a good idea." But they never give him another thought. They are like someone building a house on sand.

Jesus said that if you listen to his words and also live them out, you are like people who build their houses on the bedrock. Storms will come, winds will blow against the house, but it will stand firm. Think about this for a moment. Is there something that you have read in the Bible or this book, or heard in church or youth group, that you know you need to follow?

It may mean making some big changes. Ask Jesus to help you. Remember, if you follow him, his Spirit lives in you. You don't have to do it on your own. He will give you everything you need to be able to act upon his teaching.

Today several bridges and tunnels connect Manhattan Island to the land surrounding it. But there are other bridges in New York as well, bridges not made of steel or concrete, which have helped many to cross from where they are to somewhere better. What are these bridges? Or maybe a better question is, who are they?

Over the years, thousands of New Yorkers have worked to help the poor and disadvantaged in the city. They have reached

---

THINGS TO SEE AND DO

- High Line Park - lower West Side from Gansevoort Street to 34th Street - walk above the traffic in a park built on an old elevated train line.
- Walk the Brooklyn Bridge - entrance near City Hall at Park Row and Centre Street.

---

out in practical ways so that people could see God's love in action. And they've also told the story of how Jesus can change lives. They are like human bridges, helping people cross from spiritual darkness into the light of God's love. You might call them God's secret agents, because most of them are not well-known people. They are just quietly getting on with their work.

One of these was Lillian Kraeger. She was a member of a church in downtown New York. In 1915, two young African-American girls who lived in Harlem became followers of Jesus. They were excited about their new faith and wanted to join Lillian's church. But they were turned away. The church didn't want them because of the color of their skin.

Lillian was dismayed by this. She told the girls if they would hold Bible classes in Harlem, she would travel there and teach them. Lillian's family didn't like the idea of her teaching blacks. The man to whom she was engaged wasn't happy about it either. He told her that if she kept on going to Harlem to teach the Bible, he no longer wanted to marry her.

That must have been very hard. How would you feel if those closest to you rejected you, when all you wanted to do was reach out with Jesus' love? Lillian decided to continue with the Bible classes. She never married. Bethel Gospel Assembly Church in Harlem grew out of these classes. Today the church takes up a whole city block. Its goal is to get through to Harlem and the world beyond with the good news that Jesus can change lives.

That was also the goal of a small "army" who came from across the ocean in 1880 and landed on the southern tip of Manhattan. The soldiers were eight women known as "Hallelujah lassies" and one man. Wearing dark blue uniforms and carrying

banners, they marched down the gangplank of their steamship
and knelt on the cold ground. They gave thanks for their safe
arrival and boldly claimed the whole of America for God. A
crowd began to gather.

"Who are these people?" someone asked.

The man jumped to his feet and turned to the crowd. "Do
you know if you are bound for heaven or hell?" he asked. Then
he preached, explaining to the surprised listeners that God loved
them, and had sent Jesus to die for them. The young women got
up off their knees and joined in some rousing hymns. This was
New York's first sight of the mission known as the Salvation Army.

Fifteen years earlier in England, William Booth and his wife
Catherine had founded a mission group to reach the poor.
Instead of sitting in a church waiting for people to come to them,
they decided to go out into the streets to preach and help others.

Unlike many of God's secret agents, the Salvation Army wanted to attract attention. But not to themselves – to Jesus.

They wore uniforms, but instead of guns, their "weapons" were peace and love and the Bible. The Booths wanted to bring others to Jesus, but they knew if someone is hungry they can't think about anything but food. If they are dirty, they need a way to get clean. So their motto became the three S's: Soup, Soap, Salvation.

At street meetings listeners sometimes threw rotten vegetables and even dead rats at the Salvation Army soldiers. But this didn't discourage them. The Army put up posters inviting New Yorkers to come to street meetings to see "men who were as wild as LIONS as savage as TIGERS." These wild beasts had been "captured by Army troops and tamed."

Crowds turned up, but they didn't find wild animals. Instead they heard men tell how their lives had been turned around and tamed – not by weapons and force, but by the love and forgiveness of Jesus.

Today the Salvation Army runs about fifty social service programs in New York. They operate shelters and soup kitchens for the homeless, community centers and foster care for children, and much more. They help in many practical ways, but also try and meet spiritual needs.

It's a sad fact that New York today needs the help given by the Salvation Army and many others. If you visit the city don't be surprised if to see homeless people sleeping in doorways. Although there are lots of shelters, still thousands sleep on streets or in parks every night. About half of homeless New Yorkers are children.

Who can lend a hand? Enter God's secret agents! By their actions and words, they help people understand what God's kingdom is like.

Some of them work in offices, others in churches. Others work from home. You won't recognize them when you see them walking down the street. They look like ordinary men, women and children, but the work they do is making a big difference to New York City.

They may run soup kitchens for the hungry, provide after-school care or teach English to new immigrants. Some of them help out-of-work people train for jobs. In every small act of kindness, they show God's love. Often they tell others about Jesus, who came to earth to show God's love and forgiveness to everyone.

One of these was Mama Leo, a red-haired woman who came to New York from Puerto Rico because she felt God had told her to. She had a heart for those she called "the outcasts." Everywhere she went, she told how Jesus could change lives. She also set up programs to help people get free of alcohol and drugs. Some New Yorkers didn't like the idea of a woman doing this kind of work. Others complained about her Latina background or the fact that she worked with the lowest of society. But she kept on because she knew God had sent her.

At one point the government offered her $12 million for her programs, if she would not mention the name of Christ in her work. She supposedly replied, "You can keep your $12 million. I will keep my Christ." Many of those she helped to find Jesus have gone on to start churches and groups which minister to thousands of New Yorkers today.

Would you like to be a secret agent for God? Sometimes that will mean doing things very quietly, in the background. Often it will mean speaking out for what you believe, as Lillian Kraeger did. If you visit Bethel Gospel Assembly which she helped start, you will notice a brass plaque on the wall as you leave the church. It says, "Beyond this point lies the field." You leave the church and go outside, not into a meadow but into the streets of Harlem. This is the kind of "field" Jesus meant when he said, "Look around you! Vast fields are ripening all around us and are ready now for the harvest" (John 4:35).

Where is your harvest field? It will be found among those you live with or go to school with or play together with. Do your family and friends know Jesus? He wants you to be part of reaching them with his love. That can be scary, but he will be right there with you. Remember, the best way to tell someone about Jesus is to tell them how he has forgiven you, and the difference he has made in your life.

We've come to the end of our tour of the "city that never sleeps." I hope you've enjoyed your brief stay in this exciting place. Getting to know New York City is fun, but it doesn't compare with getting to know Jesus! That's the adventure of a lifetime, which will continue on into eternity.

New York City Map

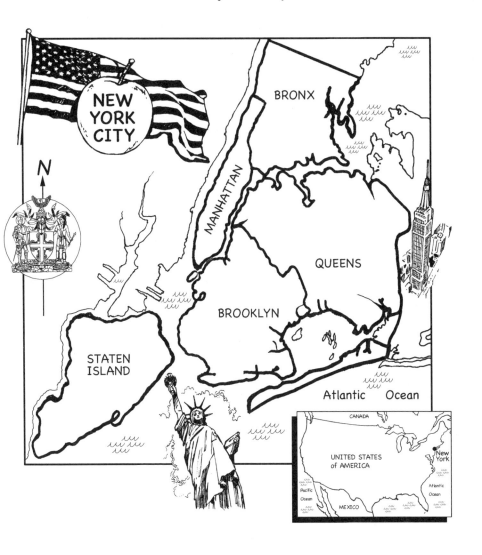

New York City Quiz

1. Who first made the phrase "The Big Apple" popular?
2. Where did the Flatiron Building get its name?
3. Can you name the five boroughs of New York City?
4. What did the Indians use tulip-poplar trees for?
5. Who said, "I regret that I have but one life to lose for my country"?
6. What word is used in the Bible for our wrong thoughts, words and actions?
7. Who took the punishment for our wrongs?
8. What was the Underground Railroad?
9. What did Sojourner Truth do?
10. How did the Fulton Street Revival start?
11. How tall is the nose on the Statue of Liberty?
12. Who called himself the Light of the World?
13. What did the "six second doctors" of Ellis Island do?
14. What was the strange humming noise heard in the Jewish Quarter of the Lower East Side?
15. Where was the only place immigrants from different countries got together?
16. Who invented the motion picture camera?
17. Where did wealthy New Yorkers build their mansions in the Gilded Age?
18. What did Jacob Riis do?
19. Why is the Empire State Building observatory closed during thunderstorms?
20. If you are a follower of Jesus, what is one way to keep your "light" shining strong?

21. How does God want us to treat those who are different from us?

22. How did the residents of Harlem escape being stared at by tourists?

23. After Jesus' death, what surprising event delighted his followers?

24. Who were the Forty Thieves and the Plug Uglies?

25. What is one way God shows he is our father?

26. How do we conquer evil, according to Romans 12:21?

27. Who traded a baseball bat for a Bible, and why?

28. How can you be like a tree?

29. Who is the most famous bird of Central Park?

30. How many eggs can the female bedbug lay?

31. What was the "miracle on the Hudson"?

32. What happens if we don't forgive others?

33. What is "caisson sickness"?

34. According to Jesus, who is like a person who builds a house on the rock?

35. What are some of the things God's "secret agents" do in New York City?

New York City Answers

1. Jazz musicians.
2. It is pointed like a clothes iron.
3. Manhattan, Brooklyn, the Bronx, Queens and Staten Island.
4. Making canoes.
5. Nathan Hale.
6. Sin.
7. Jesus, when he died on the cross.
8. A network of people and safe houses to help escaping slaves.
9. She traveled throughout the country, preaching on the rights of blacks and women.
10. With Jeremiah Lanphier holding a noon prayer meeting in a church on Fulton Street.
11. Four feet, six inches.
12. Jesus.
13. They put chalk marks on the clothes of immigrants who they suspected had disease or mental illness.
14. The sewing machines of home "sweatshop" sewing factories.
15. At the vaudeville theaters.
16. Thomas Edison.
17. On Fifth Avenue.
18. He took pictures in tenements using flash photography, and showed them to wealthy New Yorkers.
19. The building attracts lightening strikes.
20. Talking to God about everything in your life.
21. Instead of being afraid, he wants us to reach out to them in friendship.

22. They held secret "rent parties."
23. He came back from the dead in a new body.
24. Gangs of New York City.
25. By loving us, no matter what.
26. By doing good.
27. Nicky Cruz, because Jesus had forgiven him and changed his life.
28. By listening to God's teachings and living the way he says.
29. Pale Male, a red-tailed hawk.
30. Up to 500 at one time.
31. A jet with both engines out was able to land safely on the Hudson River.
32. We become bitter, which poisons our heart and leaves no room for God.
33. Also called "the bends," it occurs when divers rise too quickly to the surface.
34. The person who hears what God says and also follows it.
35. They feed the homeless, provide after-school care, teach English to immigrants and train out-of-work people for jobs.

About the Author

Donna Vann always wanted to be a writer, because books meant so much to her when she was younger. She kept notebooks of her stories, but did not begin writing books until she had three children of her own. Donna grew up in Texas. She and her husband work with an international Christian charity called Agapé Europe, and have lived in the UK for many years. She may be contacted via her website, www.donnavann.com.

The Adventures Series
An ideal series to collect

Have you ever wanted to visit the rainforest? Have you ever longed to sail down the Amazon river? Would you just love to go on Safari in Africa? Well these books can help you imagine that you are actually there. Pioneer missionaries retell their amazing adventures and encounters with animals and nature. In the Amazon you will discover tree frogs, piranha fish and electric eels. In the Rainforest you will be amazed at the armadillo and the toucan. In the blistering heat of the African Savannah you will come across lions and elephants and hyenas. And you will discover how God is at work in these amazing environments.

African Adventures by Dick Anderson
ISBN 978-1-85792-807-5
Amazon Adventures by Horace Banner
ISBN 978-1-85792-440-4
Cambodian Adventures by Donna Vann
ISBN 978-1-84550-474-8
Great Barrier Reef Adventures by Jim Cromarty
ISBN 978-1-84550-068-9
Himalayan Adventures by Penny Reeve
ISBN 978-1-84550-080-1
Kiwi Adventures by Bartha Hill
ISBN 978-1-84550-282-9
New York City Adventures by Donna Vann
ISBN 978-1-84550-546-2
Outback Adventures by Jim Cromarty
ISBN 978-1-85792-974-4
Pacific Adventures by Jim Cromarty
ISBN 978-1-84550-475-5
Rainforest Adventures by Horace Banner
ISBN 978-1-85792-627-9
Rocky Mountain Adventures by Betty Swinford
ISBN 978-1-85792-962-1
Scottish Highland Adventures by Catherine Mackenzie
ISBN 978-1-84550-281-2
Wild West Adventures by Donna Vann
ISBN 978-1-84550-065-8

CHRISTIAN FOCUS PUBLICATIONS

Christian Christian CF4K Mentor
Focus Heritage

Christian Focus Publications publishes books for adults and children under its four main imprints: Christian Focus, Christian Heritage, CF4K and Mentor. Our books reflect that God's word is reliable and Jesus is the way to know him, and live for ever with him.

Our children's publication list includes a Sunday school curriculum that covers pre-school to early teens; puzzle and activity books. We also publish personal and family devotional titles, biographies and inspirational stories that children will love.

If you are looking for quality Bible teaching for children then we have an excellent range of Bible story and age specific theological books. From pre-school to teenage fiction, we have it covered!

**Find us at our web page:
www.christianfocus.com**

CF4•K
Because you're never
too young to know Jesus